TOLKIEN'S WORLD

A FANTASY COLORING BOOK

Thunder Bay Press
An imprint of Printers Row Publishing Group
10350 Barnes Canyon Road, Suite 100, San Diego, CA 92121
www.thunderbaybooks.com

Printers Row Publishing Group is a division of Readerlink Distribution Services, LLC. The Thunder Bay Press name and logo are trademarks of Readerlink Distribution Services, LLC.

All notations of errors or omissions should be addressed to Thunder Bay Press, Editorial Department, at the above address. All other correspondence (author inquiries, permissions) concerning the content of this book should be addressed to Bounty Books, a division of Octopus Publishing Group
Carmelite House 50 Victoria Embankment
London EC4Y 0DZ
www.octopusbooks.co.uk

An Hachette UK company

Publisher: Peter Norton
Publishing Team: Lori Asbury, Ana Parker, Laura Vignale
Editorial Team: JoAnn Padgett, Melinda Allman, Dan Mansfield

ISBN: 978-1-62686-773-4

Printed in China

20 19 18 17 16 1 2 3 4 5

ABOUT THE ARTISTS

Victor Ambrus is a British illustrator also known for appearing on the Channel 4 television archaeology series *Time Team*, on which he visualized how sites under excavation may have once looked. Ambrus is an Associate of the Royal College of Art and a Fellow of both the Royal Society of Arts and the Royal Society of Painters, Etchers and Engravers.

John Davis has been an illustrator since 1960, and has worked on comics including *Thunderbirds* and *Captain Scarlett*. He has also contributed to *Rupert the Bear* annuals and began working on fantasy after reading Tolkien in 1973.

Born and raised in Milan, Mauro Mazzara started drawing at the age of two... and he still hasn't stopped! He attended the Arte & Messaggio Illustration school in Milan before studying painting at the Brera Art Academy. He now works as a freelance illustrator for the fashion, publishing, and advertising industries.

Ian Miller is a British fantasy illustrator and writer best known for his quirkily etched gothic style and macabre sensibility, and noted for his work on books by H. P. Lovecraft and contributions to David Day's Tolkien-inspired compendiums.

Andrea Piparo was born in Rome in 1990, where he graduated from art school in via Ripetta and continued his studies by attending the illustration course at the International School of Comics. He has appeared in various collective exhibitions, produced several portraits on commission, and contributed to the 2013 calendar of the Italian National Police.

WELCOME TO ARDA...

Have you ever wanted to travel through Middle-earth with Thorin and Company or the Fellowship of the Ring? Or visit the Undying Lands in the uttermost West and look upon the Trees of the Valar?

The gorgeous line art you'll find in these pages sets the scene for you to add color and detail to beloved characters and places as you've seen them in your mind a hundred times, reading *The Hobbit*, *The Silmarillion,* and *The Lord of the Rings*.

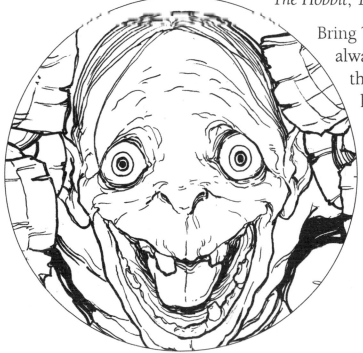

Bring Tolkien's world to life the way you've always imagined it, join the Fellowship of the Ring as they journey through perilous lands, or take up arms in the Battle of the Pelennor.

Turn the page and surround yourself with the magic of Middle-earth.

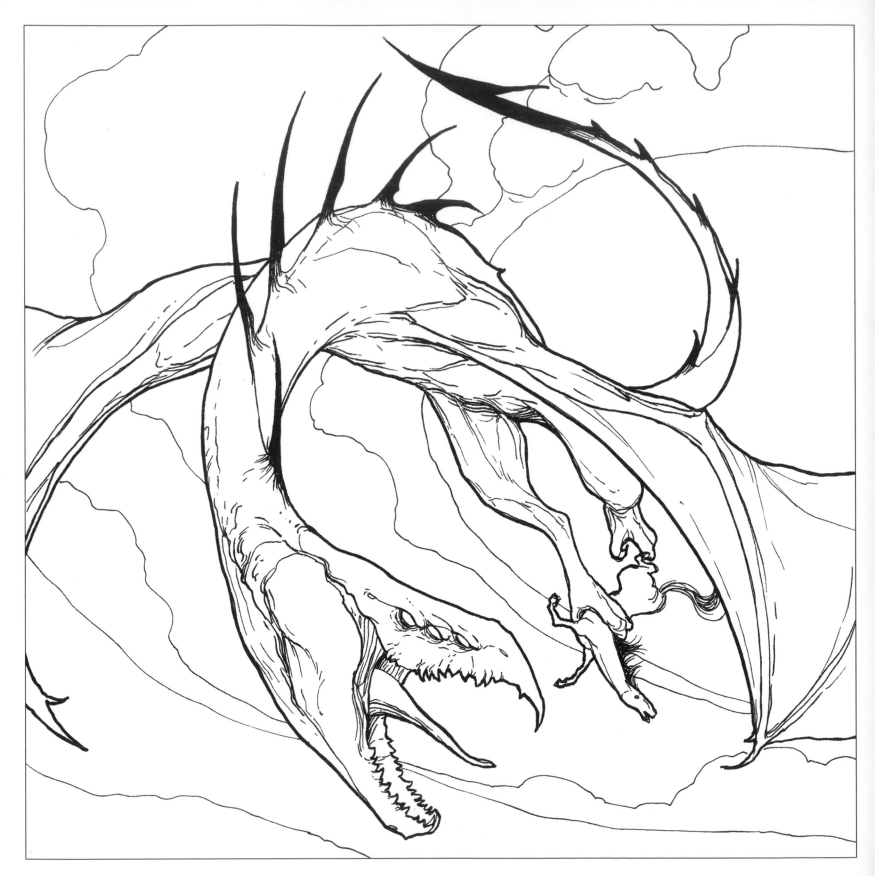

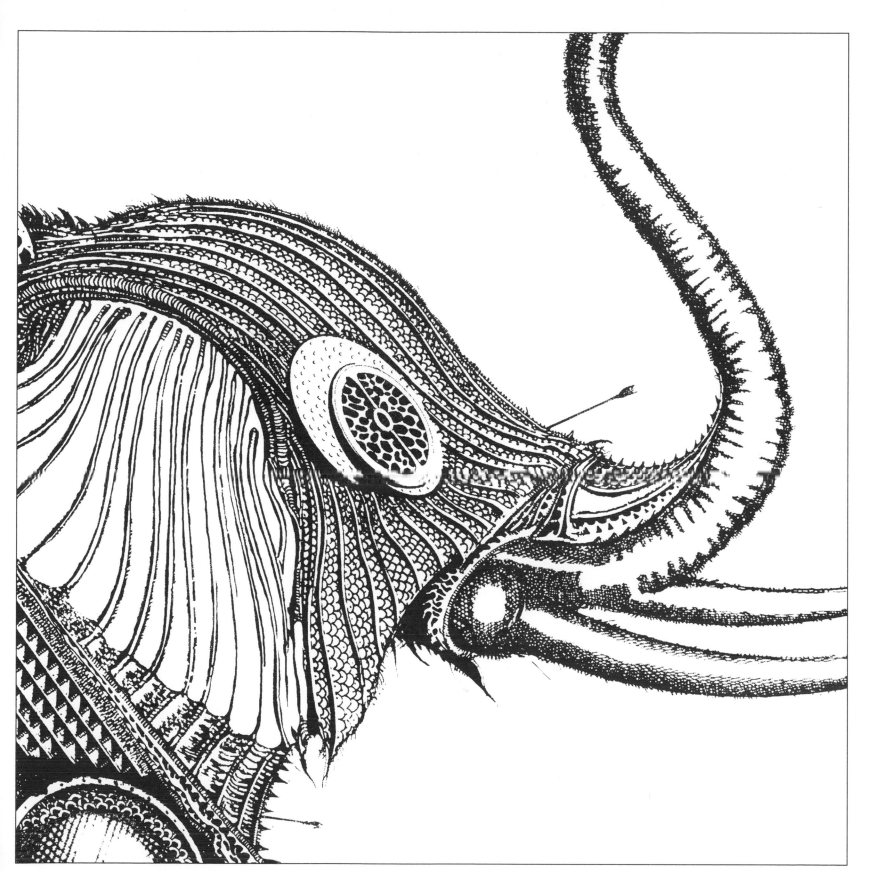

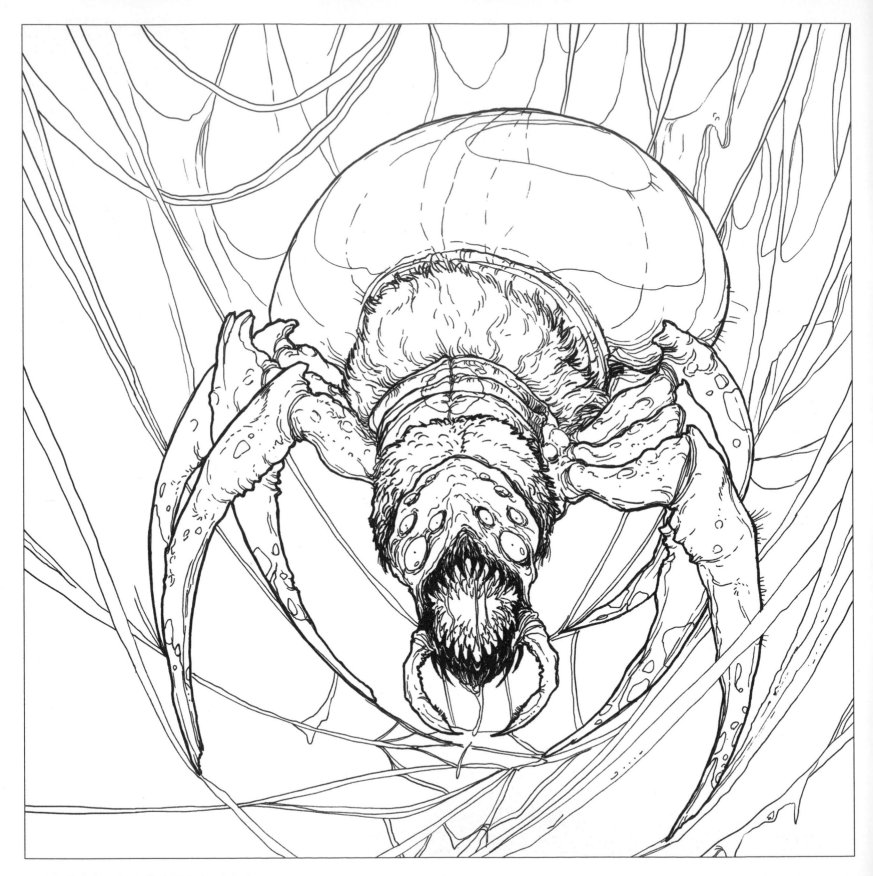

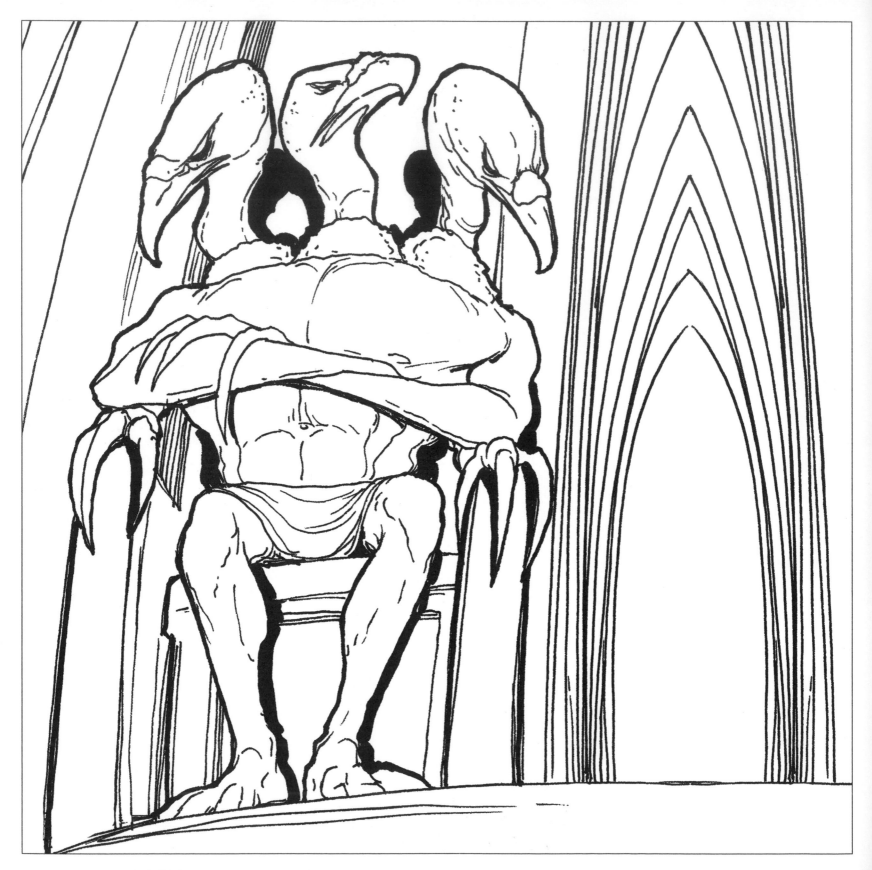